D0930470

The European Union

Political, Social, and Economic Cooperation

THE
EUROPEAN UNION

POLITICAL, SOCIAL, AND ECONOMIC COOPERATION

Austria

Belgium

Cyprus

Czech Republic

Denmark

Estonia

The European Union: Facts and Figures

Finland

France

Germany

Greece

Hungary

Ireland

Italy

Latvia

Lithuania

Luxembourg

Malta

The Netherlands

Poland

Portugal

Slovakia

Slovenia

Spain

Sweden

United Kingdom

The **European Union**

Political, Social, and Economic Cooperation

GREECE

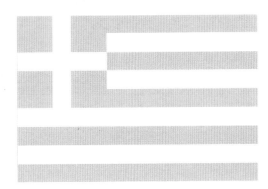

by
Kim Etingoff

Mason Crest Publishers
Philadelphia

Mason Crest Publishers Inc.
370 Reed Road
Broomall, Pennsylvania 19008
(866) MCP-BOOK (toll free)

First printing
1 2 3 4 5 6 7 8 9 10

Library of Congress Cataloging-in-Publication Data

Etingoff, Kim.
  Greece / by Kim Etingoff.
      p. cm.—(European Union: political, social, and economic cooperation)
  Audience: Ages 10+
  Includes bibliographical references and index.
    ISBN 1-4222-0049-3
    ISBN 1-4222-0038-8 (series)
  1. Greece—Juvenile literature. 2. European Union—Greece—Juvenile literature. I. Title. II. European Union (Series) (Philadelphia, Pa.)
  DF717.E75 2006
  949.5—dc22
                          2005021661

Produced by Harding House Publishing Service, Inc.
www.hardinghousepages.com
Interior design by Benjamin Stewart.
Cover design by MK Bassett-Harvey.
Printed in the Hashemite Kingdom of Jordan.

CONTENTS

GREECE
European Union Member since 1981

Dráma ●   Xánthi ●
Sirrhae ●   ● Komotiní
            Kavála ●
Thessaloníki ●

● Kastoría

Lárisa ●
● Ioánnina   ●
Trikala   Vólos ●

Lamia ●
● Agrínion
            ● Chalcis

Peiraiéfs
● Pátrai   ☆ Athens

● Kalámai

Kérkyra ●

Chaniá ●   ● Irákleton

INTRODUCTION

Sixty years ago, Europe lay scarred from the battles of the Second World War. During the next several years, a plan began to take shape that would unite the countries of the European continent so that future wars would be inconceivable. On May 9, 1950, French Foreign Minister Robert Schuman issued a declaration calling on France, Germany, and other European countries to pool together their coal and steel production as "the first concrete foundation of a European federation." "Europe Day" is celebrated each year on May 9 to commemorate the beginning of the European Union (EU).

The EU consists of twenty-five countries, spanning the continent from Ireland in the west to the border of Russia in the east. Eight of the ten most recently admitted EU member states are former communist regimes that were behind the Iron Curtain for most of the latter half of the twentieth century.

Any European country with a democratic government, a functioning market economy, respect for fundamental rights, and a government capable of implementing EU laws and policies may apply for membership. Bulgaria and Romania are set to join the EU in 2007. Croatia and Turkey have also embarked on the road to EU membership.

While the EU began as an idea to ensure peace in Europe through interconnected economies, it has evolved into so much more today:

- Citizens can travel freely throughout most of the EU without carrying a passport and without stopping for border checks.

- EU citizens can live, work, study, and retire in another EU country if they wish.

- The euro, the single currency accepted throughout twelve of the EU countries (with more to come), is one of the EU's most tangible achievements, facilitating commerce and making possible a single financial market that benefits both individuals and businesses.

- The EU ensures cooperation in the fight against cross-border crime and terrorism.

- The EU is spearheading world efforts to preserve the environment.

- As the world's largest trading bloc, the EU uses its influence to promote fair rules for world trade, ensuring that globalization also benefits the poorest countries.

- The EU is already the world's largest donor of humanitarian aid and development assistance, providing 55 percent of global official development assistance to developing countries in 2004.

The EU is neither a nation intended to replace existing nations, nor an international organization. The EU is unique—its member countries have established common institutions to which they delegate some of their sovereignty so that decisions on matters of joint interest can be made democratically at the European level.

Europe is a continent with many different traditions and languages, but with shared values such as democracy, freedom, and social justice, cherished values well known to North Americans. Indeed, the EU motto is "United in Diversity."

Enjoy your reading. Take advantage of this chance to learn more about Europe and the EU!

Ambassador John Bruton,
Head of Delegation of the European Commission, Washington, D.C.

Greece is a land of great natural beauty.

CHAPTER 1

THE LANDSCAPE

Greece is often considered the cradle of Western civilization. Its government, art, and literature have provided the foundation for the advancements of later nations and cultures. Things such as *city-states*, Homer's *The Odyssey*, and Socrates come to mind when Greece is mentioned. However, it is also a modern country, making use of new technology and providing its people with comfortable living standards.

Greece, or the Hellenic Republic as it is officially known, is located on the southern portion of the Balkan Peninsula and also includes the Peloponnesus Peninsula. The present-day country has an area of 50,942 square miles (131,940 square kilometers), roughly the size of the state of Alabama.

The Terrain:
Coastlines to Mountains

Since Greece is located on the Balkan Peninsula, the ocean surrounds it on three sides. The Aegean, Ionian, and Mediterranean seas form 8,498 miles (13,676 kilometers) of coastline stretching around the country. Greece's land boundary with other nations is only 726 miles (1,160 kilometers) long. This strategic location on the water has ruled the lives of the Greek people for all of its history, aiding in trade, military pursuits, and food.

The land that makes up Greece is extremely mountainous. The Pindus Mountains, which stretch from north to south, dominate the center of the peninsula. Much of the land is dry and very rocky, although the west has several lakes, and about 28 percent of the land is suitable for agriculture. Mountains cover over four-fifths of Greece's land, and much of the terrain is 4,920 feet (1,500 meters) above sea level. The highest mountain in the nation is the famed Mount Olympus, 9,570 feet (2,917 meters) high.

Quick Facts: The Geography of Greece

Location: Southern Europe, bordering the Aegean Sea, Ionian Sea, and the Mediterranean Sea, between Albania and Turkey
Area: slightly smaller than Alabama
  total: 50,942 square miles (131,940 sq. km.)
  land: 50,502 square miles (130,800 sq. km.)
  water: 440 square miles (1,140 sq. km.)
Borders: Albania 175 miles (282 km.), Bulgaria 307 miles (494 km.), Turkey 128 miles (206 km.), Macedonia 153 miles (246 km.)
Climate: temperate; mild, wet winters; hot, dry summers
Terrain: mostly mountains with ranges extending into the sea in the forms of peninsulas or island chains
Elevation extremes:
  lowest point: Mediterranean Sea—0 feet (0 meters)
  highest point: Mount Olympus—9,570 feet (2,917 meters)
Natural hazards: earthquakes

Source: www.cia.gov, 2005.

The Greek island of Crete is very mountainous.

ISLANDS

Much of Greece is made up of hundreds of islands, forming **archipelagos**. In fact, approximately two thousand islands surround the mainland; these islands form a fifth of Greece's total land area. There are six groups of islands, as well as two islands that do not belong to any group:

Crete and Evia. People inhabit only 169 islands; the others are too small or rocky on which to live.

CLIMATE

The surrounding presence of the sea **moderates** Greece's climate. As a result of the ocean, it has a temperate climate. Its summers are hot and dry, and its winters are mild and often wet. The northern portion of the country is somewhat cooler, especially during the winter. Neither season commonly experiences extreme temperatures, the average January temperature being 50°F (10°C) and the average temperature in July being 82°F (28°C). Snow is rare, although it sometimes falls in the higher mountains.

Windmills catch the air currents from the Mediterranean.

Animals and Plants

Greece is able to boast of a huge variety of flora and **fauna** that live within its borders. Over six thousand species of plants grow in Greece, including more than one hundred different types of orchids. Other plants such as crocuses, irises, lilies, poppies, and a large number of wild herbs also grow there. Native trees include olive, cypress, evergreen oak, juniper, and myrtle.

The mountains and the forests are home to animals like deer, badgers, lizards, lynx, and snakes. Several species of birds, especially birds of prey such as eagles and hawks, fly above Greece. Other birds include partridge, pelicans, and pheasants.

Natural Disasters

Unfortunately, Greece is subject to several types of natural disasters. The most dangerous are earthquakes and volcanoes. Earthquakes have been relatively

common in Grecian history, since the country is located on a **fault line**. The most recent earthquake occurred in 1999 in Athens.

Volcano eruptions are other looming natural disasters that threaten Greece and its citizens. Volcanic activity has a long history. The first recorded eruption of a volcano in what is now Greece was in 258 BCE, more than 2,000 years ago. Besides the fear and destruction these eruptions have caused, they have also played a role in forming many of the islands that surround Greece's mainland.

Environmental Concerns

Greece has had to face numerous threats to its environment but is working hard to counteract some of them. For example, air pollution is an urgent problem in Greece. The rise in industrial-

Sunrise over the Greek islands

ization in its cities has led to respiratory problems, damage to ancient Greek artifacts and architecture, and a disruption of the environment. The government is attempting to fight this problem by restricting the number of cars allowed into a city at one time as well as by promoting the use of cars that pollute less.

Greece's **biodiversity** is also threatened. Hunting and fishing are popular activities and have caused the loss of thousands of animals on land and in the water. People often resort to killing animals such as wolves and bears since they consider them a threat. Unfortunately, this has made these animals endangered. Other endangered species include sea turtles, dolphins, and Mediterranean monk seals, of which there are only four hundred left.

The land itself is also in danger. Though Greece was once home to vast forest lands, only parts of the north still contain these woods. Human activities like **deforestation** and forest fires have brought about the destruction of the woodlands.

Greece has a long and ancient history

2 Greece's History and Government

Greece's ancient history is familiar to many students in the Western word, but historians often debate just when the period referred to as "Ancient Greece" began. Some say it began with the first Olympic Games in 776 BCE, and some include the *prehistoric* Minoans and Mycanaeans as part of Ancient Greece. However, Ancient Greece is now usually acknowledged to have begun around 1000 BCE.

Greece's history is important to the history of the world. Greek culture influenced the later Roman Empire, which in turn directly affected Western Europe and the Americas. In order to understand Western society's beginnings, it is important to understand Greek society.

PREHISTORIC GREECE

What is now modern-day Greece was originally inhabited by a group of people known as the Minoans. The earliest recorded sign that the Minoans lived on the Balkan Peninsula dates to approximately 3000 BCE. These people were peace-loving traders who established ties with other civilizations around the world.

Around 1600 BCE, the Minoans were overtaken by a new group, the Mycenaeans. These people brought the beginning of the **Bronze Age** with them, which lasted until 1100 BCE. Decorative arts flourished, and the stage was set for later mythological writings meant to have taken place during this time. Mysteriously, the Mycenaean civilization was destroyed. Some **archaeologists** believe an invasion by the Dorians, with their superior weapons made of iron, destroyed the Mycenaean civilization.

ANCIENT DARK AGES

Whatever caused the downfall of the Mycenaeans, Greece entered a dark age. Population declined, as did education and the literacy rate. Even the language stopped being written. Cities were looted and destroyed, or abandoned and never rebuilt. Art such as pottery and jewelry lacked the **intricacy** of earlier times. The trade that had grown under the Minoans and Mycenaeans died out.

As Greece slowly emerged from this dark period, culture and civilization began to reemerge. Toward the end of the Dark Ages, **Phoenicians** reintroduced writing to the Grecians. Homer then wrote his **epics**, and other writers recorded the oral history of the time.

OFFICIAL ANCIENT GREECE: LEARNING AND WAR

The city-state (the *polis*) rose in significance during the ancient days of Greece. The two most famous were Athens and Sparta, centers of learning and advancements, although there were many other city-states. Many of the writers and philosophers that students learn about today—including Sophocles, Plato, Aristotle, and Democritus—worked during this period.

By no means did peace always remain intact through this age. Wars were often fought between city-states or between Greek alliances and an outside culture. Two of the bigger conflicts were the Persian War and the Peloponnesian War, both taking place during the 400s BCE. This last war led to the defeat of Athens and the weakening of Greece. The **Thebans**, seeing Greece's disadvantage, attacked Sparta, which had been victorious in the Peloponnesian War. Philip II of Macedon, father of Alexander the Great, entered this struggle, paving the way for Greece's empire.

THE HELLENISTIC AGE

The next stage of Greek history is called the Hellenistic period, considered to have begun with the death of Alexander the Great in 323 BCE. Alexander had begun to build an empire, including Greece, which then spread Greek culture to other areas of his empire.

The Greek god Zeus

Over the years, city-states such as Athens attempted to revolt from the empire. These attempts earned Greece limited, but valuable, results. Some southern city-states were able to gain a degree of independence from the empire. Several of these formed the Aetolian League. Unfortunately, after starting a revolt against Macedon, which controlled the empire, these city-states lost their freedoms.

ROMAN GREECE

Meanwhile, while Greece was struggling with its own wars, Rome was gaining in power. The Roman Empire eventually **annexed** Greece in 146 BCE. Roman rule did not generally affect the average Grecian. The area's culture was left alone, and local governments were allowed to function as normally as possible. Despite this freedom, Roman rule did have some impact on Greece, and city-states were required to pay **tribute** to the empire. But Greece even gained from the Romans: all free males in the empire were given the right to vote.

THE BYZANTINE EMPIRE

After the division of the Roman Empire, Greece became part of the Eastern, or Byzantine, Empire. During this period, Greek life followed the ups and downs of the empire as a whole. Orthodox Christianity became an increasing presence, and wars were fought between the Byzantine Empire and outsiders.

During this time, the people of the Balkan Peninsula began to form a firmer idea of Greek identity. Although the area was relatively poor after joining the Byzantine Empire, it gained a more unified Greek way of life, including a common language and religion.

OTTOMAN RULE

In 1453 CE, the Byzantine Empire fell to the Ottomans, a Turkish group of people, and the Byzantine period ended. To avoid Ottoman rule, the Greeks took action in the form of migration. Some traveled to Western Europe, while others moved from the plains of Greece to the mountains. The Greeks who ended up under Turkish rule resented it. Greeks often became Crypto-Christians, or those who practiced Turkish Islam but were secretly Christian. Those who actually converted to Islam were sometime **ostracized** by other Greeks who believed the new Muslims were abandoning their Greek heritage.

In 1821, the Greeks began to fight for independence, which they gained in 1829. A republic was initially established but became a monarchy in 1833.

GREECE ENTERS THE MODERN WORLD

During World War I, Greece fought on the side of the Allies against the Central Powers, including Turkey. After the war, Greece was given small amounts of land in return for its help.

A Roman stadium outside Athens

In World War II, Greece again sided with the Allied Powers, although it had little to offer with its small number of troops. Italy invaded Greece in 1940, but Greece earned the first Allied victory of WWII when it defeated Italian forces. Eventually, the Axis Powers overwhelmed Greece and occupied the country. Thousands of people were killed, some in concentration camps, others

The church played on ongoing role in Greek history.

in battle. Jews were especially hunted by the occupying Germans, although the Greek Orthodox Church tried to save many.

The aftermath of WWII did not see much improvement for the Greeks. Greece's economy had been destroyed during the war and occupation. Many Greeks believed it was time for a change in government. A civil war was fought in 1949 between royalists who supported the king and **communists**.

Greece's government during the 1960s and 1970s was anything but stable. In 1967, a **coup** overthrew the government and set up the Regime of the Colonels, which forced the king into **exile**. Many believed the United States was involved in this action. An election in 1974 disbanded the monarchy and set up a democratic constitution the following year.

GREECE TODAY

Democracy has continued to thrive in Greece. The country's government consists of the elected president, elected for a five-year term; the 300-member parliament; and the judiciary system. Voting is universal over the age of eighteen.

Greece's economy is still growing. The country joined the European Union (EU) in 1981 and hosted the Olympic Games in 2004. Although the Olympic Games were not a financial success, they did bring new attention to this ancient country. It is now enjoying tourism and new technology that has brought Greece into the twenty-first century.

Tourists flock to Greece's seaside towns, enriching the Greek economy.

3 THE ECONOMY

As in most countries today, Greece's economy has been changing, shifting from agriculture, to industry, to service. Fortunately, the country has been able to keep up with the changing world and has a stable and prosperous economy.

One of Greece's many open-air markets

THE CHANGING ROLE OF AGRICULTURE AND INDUSTRY

Agriculture has always been an important part of the Greek economy. However, after the mid-1900s, it began to decline because of the rise in industrial activity. While Greece used to rely almost entirely on exporting agricultural products, it now adds industrial goods to its export list. Greece produces such crops as cotton, grapes, olives, tobacco, and vegetables. Sheep and goats are two of its most important livestock outputs.

Greece began to develop its industries after World War II. This was due to foreign aid and sup-

portive government policies. Industry contributes 22 percent to Greece's **gross domestic product (GDP)**, second to the service industry. Processed foods, clothing, chemicals, and cement are Greece's primary industries. Mining is another source of Greece's exports. Bauxite, nickel, iron ore, asbestos, and marble are all found below the earth and mined extensively.

EMPLOYERS

The government provides many jobs to the Greek people. Since the government owns and runs many institutions, like banks, schools, and hospitals, it must employ people to work there. A large percentage of the people also work for businesses owned by government banks.

Those not employed by the government often work for them-

selves. Traditional family businesses are still a big part of the Greek economy, as is self-employment in newer businesses. The **entrepreneurial** spirit runs high in Greece.

QUICK FACTS: THE ECONOMY OF GREECE

Gross Domestic Product (GDP): US$226.4 billion
GDP per capita: US$21,300
Industries: tourism; food and tobacco processing, textiles; chemicals, metal products; mining, petroleum
Agriculture: wheat, corn, barley, sugar beets, olives, tomatoes, wine, tobacco, potatoes; beef, dairy products
Export commodities: food and beverages, manufactured goods, petroleum products, chemicals, textiles
Export partners: Germany 13.3%, Italy 10.2%, UK 7.6%, Bulgaria 6.5%, U.S. 5.2%, Cyprus 4.6%, Turkey 4.6%, France 4.2%
Import commodities: machinery, transport equipment, fuels, chemicals
Import partners: Germany 13.3%, Italy 12.6%, France 6.6%, Russia 5.4%, Netherlands 5.4%, South Korea 4.6%, U.S. 4.2%, U.K. 4.1%
Currency: euro
Currency exchange rate: US$1 = €.82 euro (July 21, 2005)

Note: All figures are from 2004 unless otherwise noted.
Source: www.cia.gov, 2005.

A Country for Tourists

The ancient history and art, as well as the beaches, of Greece have long proved to be attractive to people around the world. Tourism has provided a big boost to the Greek economy during the last few decades and now accounts for a large part of the country's GDP. The service industry, of which tourism is a part, makes up 69 percent of the GDP. Hotels have been built, local arts and crafts sold, and transportation improved to accommodate the growing number of tourists.

Transportation

Greece has a public transportation system that allows visitors and inhabitants to travel around the cities, as well as the whole country. Buses and trains are the two most popular and most extensive systems on land. Athens has a subway system as well. Ferries travel between Greece's many islands.

Greece also has a number of airports, both international and ***domestic***. Olympic Airways and Aegean Airlines offer transportation between Greece's larger cities. International airports are located in Athens and Thessaloníki.

Roads in Greece are usually paved and modern. Six thousand miles (9,656 kilometers) of roads have been classified as national highways, connecting different parts of the country.

ENERGY

Greece's abundant coal supply provides the country with two-thirds of its energy. Greece also uses oil, but since it does not have this particular resource within its borders, it must import it. Because of its thousands of miles of coastline, Greece is able to **exploit** the energy from the sea, converting the action of the waves into hydroelectric power, which provides 6 percent of Greece's electricity.

The sea plays an imprtant role in Greece's culture.

4 GREECE'S PEOPLE AND CULTURE

Greece is a very **homogeneous** society; 98 percent of its citizens are ethnic Greeks, with the remaining 2 percent being mainly comprised of Turks and illegal immigrants, especially Albanians. As a result, although it lacks diversity, Greece is a unified country in which its people share a common culture.

In the 1950s and 1960s, a large number of Greeks left their country for those of Western Europe. Approximately 10 percent left their homes in Greece in order to escape the troubled times in their country. When times calmed, many returned to their homeland.

LANGUAGE

Unlike countries where there is more **diversity** in the population, most Greeks speak the same language. Modern Greek differs from the language of Ancient Greece, but they do share the same alphabet.

In addition to Greek, many people are able to speak German and English. Minorities are sometimes heard to speak Turkish, Macedonian, or Albanian.

RELIGION

Another unifying force in Greek life is the Greek Orthodox Church. Those same 98 percent of citizens who are Greek also practice this religion. Interestingly, of these people, 10 percent are Old Calendarists, meaning that they use the old Julian calendar instead of the modern Gregorian one. Islam is the next most practiced religion, followed by Roman Catholicism.

Religion plays an integral role in Greek holidays and festivals. Easter is especially important in Greek religious life, as well as the Feast of the Dormition, or Assumption.

QUICK FACTS: THE PEOPLE OF GREECE

Population: 10,668,354
Ethnic groups: Greek 98%, other 2%
Age structure:
  0–14 years: 14.4%
  15–64 years: 66.8%
  65 years and over: 18.8%
Population growth rate: 0.19%
Birth rate: 9.72 births/1,000 pop.
Death rate: 10.15/deaths/1,000 pop.
Migration rate: 2.34 migrant(s)/1,000 pop.
Infant mortality rate: 5.53 deaths/1,000 live births
Life expectancy at birth:
  Total population: 79.09 years
  Male: 76.59 years
  Female: 81.76 years
Total fertility rate: 1.33 children born/woman
Religions: Greek Orthodox 98%, Muslim 1.3%, other 0.7%
Languages: Greek 99%, English, French
Literacy rate: 96.5% (2003)

Note: All figures are from 2005 unless otherwise noted.
Source: www.cia.gov, 2005.

Greek cuisine

EDUCATION

Greeks place much importance on education and work hard to provide a good education for students. School attendance is **compulsory** until age fourteen, when it becomes optional to continue. It is free at all times. Students who continue their education tend to get better jobs in Greece, since many employers require their workers to have had attended school past the age of fourteen.

There are no private universities, so competition for acceptance is tight for those wanting to attend the small number of public universities. Some students attend unofficial private schools that offer higher education or study outside of Greece.

SPORTS: THE EFFECTS OF THE OLYMPICS

True to their history of hosting the original Olympic Games, Greeks continue to participate in sports. Soccer (or football, as it's called in Europe) and basketball are popular. The popularity of basketball is very unusual, since it is not so prominent in other European countries.

At the Olympics themselves, Greece has reason to be proud. It hosted the first modern Olympics in 1896 and has since produced many medal-winning athletes. In 2004, Athens again hosted the Olympics, and many stadiums and other accommodations were built especially for the games.

The ruins of ancient Greek architecture

FOOD

From cafes to restaurants, Greeks love to eat their favorite foods out of their own kitchens. Cafes, or *kafeneias*, are popular places to eat pastries or drink a cup of coffee. Once they were open only to men, but that is now changing. Other places, like tavernas, are informal restaurants suitable for eating a full meal.

In restaurants and at home, Greek cuisine shows the influence that Turkey has had on the country. *Souvlaki* (meat in pita bread), *tzatziki* (cucumber and yogurt dip), and *spanikopita* (spinach in filo dough) are traditional dishes of Turkish origin. Desserts include *baklava* and *kadayifi*, both made with large amounts of honey, typical in most desserts.

LITERATURE: PAST AND PRESENT

Many of Greek's writers are famous in the Western world, and their works, often referred to as the Classics. Many are required reading in school. The most well known, Homer, wrote *The Illiad* and *The Odyssey*. Other writers include the poet Sappho, who wrote love poems, and Pausanias, the world's first travel writer.

Although Greek literature is often dominated by the writers of ancient times, the country also boasts well-written modern works. Two Greek poets, Odysseus Elytis and George Seferis, won the Nobel Prize for literature during the 1900s. Other writers, such as novelist Nikos Kazantzakis, are famous in Greece and becoming better known in other parts of the world.

Art and Architecture

Throughout the long history of Greece, the art of the area has changed with the age and with the people. Greek art even directly influenced Roman art forms. Sculptures of ancient Greece often depicted human figures or myths. One theme that has remained the same is the Greeks' love of painted pottery, with designs ranging from figures to geometric patterns.

Few examples remain of Ancient Greek architecture; what have survived are mostly temples such as the Temple of Hephaestus and the Parthenon, created by the Greek architect Iktinos. Additionally, many theaters, which were important centers in towns, have survived.

Greek art is not all ancient. More modern artists include El Greco (Domenikos Theotokopoulos) from the island of Crete, who spent most of his life painting in Spain during the 1500s.

Music and Dance

Traditional forms of music tend to be popular among Greeks, even with the younger generations. One such example is *rebetika* music, which contains messages about suffering and poverty.

Dances often accompany music, especially at family celebrations and events. The *hasapiko*, *kalamatiano*, and *tsamiko* are all common Greek dances. As in other areas of culture, dances show traditions imported from Turkey.

Athens' ancient architecture draws tourists from around the world.

5 THE CITIES

CHAPTER

After World War II, urbanization, or the movement of people from rural areas to cities, increased. Today, over 60 percent of Greeks live in urban areas, with one-third of the entire population living in Athens alone.

ATHENS

Athens has long been an important part of Greece. From a major city-state, it has transformed into the country's capital. It was named for Athena, the Greek goddess of wisdom.

This city is the site of many important examples of Greek art and architecture, including the Parthenon, the Acropolis, and the chapel of Ai Giorgis. Its many museums house Greek sculptures and paintings.

Athens is one of the most diverse places in Greece. Many of the country's immigrants, as well as millions of ethnic Greeks, call Athens home. This ethnic diversity, coupled with the culture present in Athens, makes this city a popular destination for tourists. A large portion of the local population has been provided with jobs, and the city's modernization can be traced to Athens' reputation as a tourist destination.

THESSALONÍKI

The second-largest city in Greece is the capital of the northern region of Macedonia. Thessaloníki is a very fashionable city, filled with cafes, clubs, and shops. The Thessaloníki Film Festival in the autumn is a famous attraction for people all over the world.

The city also has its share of ancient culture, like the tomb of Philip of Macedon, father of Alexander the Great. There are many Roman and Byzantine ruins as well, reflecting its long history

Piraeus is Athens' port city.

beginning from its founding in 316 BCE. Newer, but no less important, is the White Tower, the symbol of the city built in the fifteenth century, which sits close to the local university.

PIRAEUS

Sitting just south of Athens, Piraeus has served as that city's most important port, both in ancient days and in modern times. Its location on the Mediterranean Sea provides ferry access to and from several islands, including Crete. The port also allows for cargo brought into and out of Athens.

Although Piraeus is a city focused on industrialization, it still attracts tourists because of its close proximity to Athens and the sea. Its city center, filled with Greek charm, also lures visitors.

PÁTRAI

Pátrai, or Patras, is the largest city on the southern Peloponnesian Peninsula and a major port that provides a gateway from Greece to Italy, and to the many islands surrounding the mainland. Pátrai's Carnival in February is one of the most famous and lively in the country.

The main portion of the city sits below an old castle that dominates the area. Surrounding the castle are restaurants, parks, and shops. Pátrai also has the Cathedral of St. Andrew, the city's patron saint.

OLYMPIA

Although Olympia is not a major Greek city, it is the namesake of the Olympic Games. As early as 1000 BCE, the games were an exciting local event. By 776 BCE, the games had spread to cities around Greece. Today, Olympia is the starting point from which the Olympic torch begins its journey around the world. It is also the headquarters for the modern Olympic Games.

The EU flag

6

THE FORMATION OF THE EUROPEAN UNION

The EU is an economic and political confederation of twenty-five European nations. Member countries abide by common foreign and security policies and cooperate on judicial and domestic affairs. The confederation, however, does not replace existing states or governments. Each of the twenty-five member states is **autonomous**, but they have all agreed to establish some common institutions and to hand over some of their own decision-making powers to these international bodies. As a result, decisions on matters that interest all member states can be made democratically, accommodating everyone's concerns and interests.

Today, the EU is the most powerful regional organization in the world. It has evolved from a primarily economic organization to an increasingly political one. Besides promoting economic cooperation, the EU requires that its members uphold fundamental values of peace and **solidarity**, human dignity, freedom, and equality. Based on the principles of democracy and the rule of law, the EU respects the culture and organizations of member states.

HISTORY

The seeds of the EU were planted more than fifty years ago in a Europe reduced to smoking piles of rubble by two world wars. European nations suffered great financial difficulties in the postwar period. They were struggling to get back on their feet and realized that another war would cause further hardship. Knowing that internal conflict was hurting all of Europe, a drive began toward European cooperation.

France took the first historic step. On May 9, 1950 (now celebrated as Europe Day), Robert Schuman, the French foreign minister, proposed the coal and steel industries of France and West Germany be coordinated under a single supranational authority. The proposal, known as the Treaty of Paris, attracted four other countries—Belgium, Luxembourg, the Netherlands, and Italy—and resulted in the 1951 formation of the European Coal and Steel Community (ECSC). These six countries became the founding members of the EU.

In 1957, European cooperation took its next big leap. Under the Treaty of Rome, the European Economic Community (EEC) and the European Atomic Energy Community (EURATOM) were formed. Informally known as the Common Market, the EEC promoted joining the national economies into a single European economy. The 1965 Treaty of Brussels (more commonly referred to as the Merger Treaty) united these various treaty organizations under a single umbrella, the European Community (EC).

In 1992, the Maastricht Treaty (also known as the Treaty of the European Union) was signed in Maastricht, the Netherlands, signaling the birth of the EU as it stands today. **Ratified** the following year, the Maastricht Treaty provided f banking system, a common currency (replace the national currencies, a leg of the EU, and a framework for exp

The EU's united economy has allowed it to become a worldwide financial power.

EU's political role, particularly in the area of foreign and security policy.

By 1993, the member countries completed their move toward a single market and agreed to participate in a larger common market, the European Economic Area, established in 1994.

The EU, headquartered in Brussels, Belgium, reached its current member strength in spurts. In

1973, Denmark, Ireland, and the United Kingdom joined the six founding members of the EC. They were followed by Greece in 1981, and Portugal and Spain in 1986. The 1990s saw the unification of the two Germanys, and as a result, East Germany entered the EU fold. Austria, Finland, and Sweden joined the EU in 1995, bringing the total number of member states to fifteen. In 2004, the EU nearly doubled its size when ten countries—Cyprus, the Czech Republic, Estonia, Hungary, Latvia, Lithuania, Malta, Poland, Slovakia, and Slovenia—became members.

THE EU FRAMEWORK

The EU's structure has often been compared to a "roof of a temple with three columns." As established by the Maastricht Treaty, this three-pillar framework encompasses all the policy areas—or pillars—of European cooperation. The three pillars of the EU are the European Community, the Common Foreign and Security Policy (CFSP), and Police and Judicial Co-operation in Criminal Matters.

QUICK FACTS: THE EUROPEAN UNION

Number of Member Countries: 25
Official Languages: 20—Czech, Danish, Dutch, English, Estonian, Finnish, French, German, Greek, Hungarian, Italian, Latvian, Lithuanian, Maltese, Polish, Portuguese, Slovak, Slovenian, Spanish, and Swedish; additional language for treaty purposes: Irish Gaelic
Motto: *In Varietate Concordia* (United in Diversity)
European Council's President: Each member state takes a turn to lead the council's activities for 6 months.
European Commission's President: José Manuel Barroso (Portugal)
European Parliament's President: Josep Borrell (Spain)
Total Area: 1,502,966 square miles (3,892,685 sq. km.)
Population: 454,900,000
Population Density: 302.7 people/square mile (116.8 people/sq. km.)
GDP: €9.61.1012
Per Capita GDP: €21,125
Formation:

- Declared: February 7, 1992, with signing of the Maastricht Treaty
- Recognized: November 1, 1993, with the ratification of the Maastricht Treaty

Community Currency: Euro. Currently 12 of the 25 member states have adopted the euro as their currency.
Anthem: "Ode to Joy"
Flag: Blue background with 12 gold stars arranged in a circle
Official Day: Europe Day, May 9

Source: europa.eu.int

The European Community pillar deals with economic, social, and environmental policies. It is a body consisting of the European Parliament, European Commission, European Court of Justice, Council of the European Union, and the European Courts of Auditors.

The idea that the EU should speak with one voice in world affairs is as old as the European integration process itself. Toward this end, the Common Foreign and Security Policy (CFSP) was formed in 1993.

Pillar Three

The cooperation of EU member states in judicial and criminal matters ensures that its citizens enjoy the freedom to travel, work, and live securely and safely anywhere within the EU. The third pillar—Police and Judicial Co-operation in Criminal Matters—helps to protect EU citizens from international crime and to ensure equal access to justice and fundamental rights across the EU.

The flags of the EU's nations:

top row, left to right
Belgium, the Czech Republic, Denmark, Germany, Estonia, Greece

second row, left to right
Spain, France, Ireland, Italy, Cyprus, Latvia

third row, left to right
Lithuania, Luxembourg, Hungary, Malta, the Netherlands, Austria

bottom row, left to right
Poland, Portugal, Slovenia, Slovakia, Finland, Sweden, United Kingdom

Economic Status

As of May 2004, the EU had the largest economy in the world, followed closely by the United States. But even though the EU continues to enjoy a trade surplus, it faces the twin problems of high unemployment rates and **stagnancy**.

The 2004 addition of ten new member states is expected to boost economic growth. EU membership is likely to stimulate the economies of these relatively poor countries. In turn, their prosperity growth will be beneficial to the EU.

The Euro

The EU's official currency is the euro, which came into circulation on January 1, 2002. The shift to the euro has been the largest monetary changeover in the world. Twelve countries—Belgium, Germany, Greece, Spain, France, Ireland, Italy, Luxembourg, the Netherlands, Finland, Portugal, and Austria—have adopted it as their currency.

Single Market

Within the EU, laws of member states are harmonized and domestic policies are coordinated to create a larger, more-efficient single market.

The chief features of the EU's internal policy on the single market are:

- free trade of goods and services

- a common EU competition law that controls anticompetitive activities of companies and member states

- removal of internal border control and harmonization of external controls between member states

- freedom for citizens to live and work anywhere in the EU as long as they are not dependent on the state

- free movement of **capital** between member states

- harmonization of government regulations, corporation law, and trademark registration

- a single currency

- coordination of environmental policy

- a common agricultural policy and a common fisheries policy

- a common system of indirect taxation, the value-added tax (VAT), and common customs duties and **excise**

- funding for research

- funding for aid to disadvantaged regions

The EU's external policy on the single market specifies:

- a common external **tariff** and a common position in international trade negotiations

- funding of programs in other Eastern European countries and developing countries

COOPERATION AREAS

EU member states cooperate in other areas as well. Member states can vote in European Parliament elections. Intelligence sharing and cooperation in criminal matters are carried out through EUROPOL and the Schengen Information System.

The EU is working to develop common foreign and security policies. Many member states are resisting such a move, however, saying these are sensitive areas best left to individual member states. Arguing in favor of a common approach to security and foreign policy are countries like France and Germany, who insist that a safer and more secure Europe can only become a reality under the EU umbrella.

One of the EU's great achievements has been to create a boundary-free area within which people, goods, services, and money can move around freely; this ease of movement is sometimes called "the four freedoms." As the EU grows in size, so do the challenges facing it—and yet its fifty-year history has amply demonstrated the power of cooperation.

The EU believes that it can use its power to act as a "lighthouse" for the rest of the world.

Key EU Institutions

Five key institutions play a specific role in the EU.

The European Parliament

The European Parliament (EP) is the democratic voice of the people of Europe. Directly elected every five years, the Members of the European Parliament (MEPs) sit not in national **blocs** but in political groups representing the seven main political parties of the member states. Each group reflects the political ideology of the national parties to which its members belong. Some MEPs are not attached to any political group.

Council of the European Union

The Council of the European Union (formerly known as the Council of Ministers) is the main leg-

islative and decision-making body in the EU. It brings together the nationally elected representatives of the member-state governments. One minister from each of the EU's member states attends council meetings. It is the forum in which government representatives can assert their interests and reach compromises. Increasingly, the Council of the European Union and the EP are acting together as colegislators in decision-making processes.

EUROPEAN COMMISSION

The European Commission does much of the day-to-day work of the EU. Politically independent, the commission represents the interests of the EU as a whole, rather than those of individual member states. It drafts proposals for new European laws, which it presents to the EP and the Council of the European Union. The European ...sion makes sure EU decisions are imple- properly and supervises the way EU ...re spent. It also sees that everyone abides ...uropean treaties and European law. ...EU member-state governments choose the ...an Commission president, who is then ...d by the EP. Member states, in consulta- ...h the incoming president, nominate the ...ropean Commission members, who must ...approved by the EP. The commission is

appointed for a five-year term, but can be dismissed by the EP. Many members of its staff work in Brussels, Belgium.

COURT OF JUSTICE

Headquartered in Luxembourg, the Court of Justice of the European Communities consists of one independent judge from each EU country. This court ensures that the common rules decided in the EU are understood and followed uniformly by all the members. The Court of Justice settles disputes over how EU treaties and legislation are interpreted. If national courts are in doubt about how to apply EU rules, they must ask the Court of Justice. Individuals can also bring proceedings against EU institutions before the court.

COURT OF AUDITORS

EU funds must be used legally, economically, and for their intended purpose. The Court of Auditors, an independent EU institution located in Luxembourg, is responsible for overseeing how EU money is spent. In effect, these auditors help European taxpayers get better value for the money that has been channeled into the EU.

OTHER IMPORTANT BODIES

1. European Economic and Social Committee: expresses the opinions of organized civil society on economic and social issues

2. Committee of the Regions: expresses the opinions of regional and local authorities

3. European Central Bank: responsible for monetary policy and managing the euro

4. European Ombudsman: deals with citizens' complaints about mismanagement by any EU institution or body

5. European Investment Bank: helps achieve EU objectives by financing investment projects

Together with a number of agencies and other bodies completing the system, the EU's institutions have made it the most powerful organization in the world.

EU Member States

In order to become a member of the EU, a country must have a stable democracy that guarantees the rule of law, human rights, and protection of minorities. It must also have a functioning market economy as well as a civil service capable of applying and managing EU laws.

The EU provides substantial financial assistance and advice to help candidate countries prepare themselves for membership. As of October 2004, the EU has twenty-five member states. Bulgaria and Romania are likely to join in 2007, which would bring the EU's total population to nearly 500 million.

In December 2004, the EU decided to open negotiations with Turkey on its proposed membership. Turkey's possible entry into the EU has been fraught with controversy. Much of this controversy has centered on Turkey's human rights record and the divided island of Cyprus. If allowed to join the EU, Turkey would be its most-populous member state.

The 2004 expansion was the EU's most ambitious enlargement to date. Never before has the EU embraced so many new countries, grown so much in terms of area and population, or encompassed so many different histories and cultures. As the EU moves forward into the twenty-first century, it will undoubtedly continue to grow in both political and economic strength.

The bay at Patmos

7 GREECE IN THE EUROPEAN UNION

Greece is neither a founding member nor a very new member to the EU. In 1981, Greece became the tenth nation to join the European Economic Community (EEC). Ten years later, in 1991, it was one of the twelve countries to sign the Maastricht Treaty, officially forming the EU.

THE EURO

In 1999, a new monetary unit, the euro, was introduced to several members of the EU. The Greek government had worked to introduce it to the country, forcing the high inflation rate down and increasing taxes. Despite these unpopular policies, Greece was unable to meet the qualifications to adopt the euro.

Greece continued working toward acceptance of the euro and finally met the goal set by the EU in 2000. The euro was then put into circulation in 2001.

HELP FROM, AND FOR, THE EU

During the first decade after the formation of the EU, Greece relied heavily on money from the organization. From 1994 to 1999, almost $20 billion was given to Greece just to prepare for the 2004 Olympics in Athens. Existing transportation systems were improved and new ones built, specifically a subway network and a new international airport. Other funds have been used for improving living conditions and the economy.

In addition, the EU has worked with Greece to **liberalize** its economic policies. For example, over the past few years, the Greek government eliminated many restrictions it had placed on the country's banking system. Now, more banks are able to operate with less government intrusion.

As Greece has progressed under the EU, it has been able to offer its services to the organi-

Life in modern-day Greece reflects the traditions of the past.

Sunset over the island of Patmos

zation. In the first half of 2003, it took on the EU presidency. Greece also contributes close to 2 percent of the total EU budget, a number in accordance with the total population of the EU that is Greek.

INTERGOVERNMENTALISM VS. SUPRANATIONALISM

Currently, a debate is going on within the EU. On one side are smaller and less powerful nations that support intergovernmentalism, a term used to describe a policy of making decisions based on agreement by all members of the EU. Smaller countries believe this protects their right to have a say in all EU decisions.

On the other hand, larger countries tend to support supranationalism, which means decisions are made by a majority of votes by elected representatives. Supporters of this method feel that under intergovernmentalism, decisions would be delayed waiting for all EU member states to agree.

Greece is a proponent of intergovernmentalism. It is interested in allowing all nations, including itself and other small countries, to participate in the EU at all times. It also believes that by adopting intergovernmentalism, member states can protect their own identities and rights in favor of a giant EU community.

GREECE'S FUTURE IN THE EU

Since Greece has come such a long way during the more than two decades it has belonged to a

European community, the EU is planning to slowly stop giving Greece funds for improvement. By 2006, the last structural funds will be given to Greece.

Greece's involvement in the EU may have given the country's foreign relations a positive boost. Historically, the relationship between Greece and Turkey has been strained. However, that is slowly changing. In 1999, Greece was one of the first countries to send aid to Turkey after an earthquake. After another earthquake, this time in Greece, Turkey then helped out its Greek neighbors. Greece is now supporting Turkey in its effort to join the EU.

Hopefully, the EU will provide a stage for Greece to further improve its relations with EU member states and other European countries. The future looks bright for Greece if it continues to complement its ancient heritage with its cooperation within the EU.

A Calendar of Greek Festivals

January: New Year's Day is a religious holiday in Greece, called the **Feast of Saint Basil**. Gifts are given to children and church is attended. In the north, **Gynaikratia**, celebrated on the January 8, is a fun holiday in which men and women switch places in society. Men work at home while women eat in cafes or spend time in other traditional men's places.

February/March: In the three weeks before Lent, **Carnival season** is a time for food, dancing, and music. **Easter**, which follows it, is a much more solemn holiday. It is the most important celebration of the Greek Orthodox Church and is observed with candle-lit processions, church services, and feasts. **Greek Independence Day**, March 25, celebrates the beginning of the Greek rebellion against Turkey and includes military parades.

April: On April 23, the **Feast of St. George**, a patron saint of many villages, is observed.

August: The day of the **Assumption of the Virgin Mary**, August 15, includes feasts, pilgrimages, and parades.

October: The **National Anniversary of Greek Independence**, on the 28th, is also called "Ohi Day" in memory of a general's resistance to Italian occupation during World War II.

December: Christmas is a religious holiday celebrated on December 25, but is increasingly becoming more secular under Western influences.

Greek Lemon Soup

Serves 4

Ingredients
1 quart chicken stock
5 ounces long grain rice
3 egg yolks
2 ounces lemon juice
salt and pepper
4 thin slices lemon to garnish
freshly chopped parsley to garnish

Directions
In a large saucepan, bring the chicken stock to a boil. Add the rice, and stir well. Reduce the heat, cover, and simmer for about 20 minutes or until the rice is tender.

In a small bowl, whisk together the egg yolks and lemon juice until well blended. Once rice is cooked, remove from heat and add about 8 ounces of the hot soup to the egg and lemon mixture and whisk vigorously to combine (you are tempering the egg so it doesn't scramble). Pour the egg/soup mixture back into the saucepan, whisking constantly until well blended. Over medium heat, bring the soup to a simmer, stirring constantly. Do not boil or it will curdle. Season with salt and pepper to taste and serve immediately. Garnish with the lemon slices and parsley.

Souvlaki

Serves 6

Ingredients
2 pounds of pork fillet, cut into 1-inch cubes
1 tablespoon olive oil
1 tablespoon freshly chopped oregano
salt and pepper
extra olive oil
6 pita breads
juice of 4 lemons
tzaziki to serve (see recipe)

Directions
In a large bowl, mix together the pork, oregano, olive oil, salt, and pepper. Thread the meat cubes onto skewers and grill for 7 to 10 minutes on each side, or until cooked through.

Brush the pitas with a little olive oil and place under the grill to lightly brown and heat through. Once the meat is cooked, place the lemon juice in a tall glass or shallow container and coat the cooked pork on all sides with the lemon juice. Remove the pork from the skewers and divide between the pita pockets. Sprinkle with salt and add a spoonful of tzaziki. Serve immediately.

Tzatziki

Serves 4–8

Ingredients
1 large cucumber
4 garlic cloves, crushed
salt and white pepper
squeeze of lemon juice
10 ounces plain yogurt
1 tablespoon olive oil
1 tablespoon finely chopped fresh mint

Directions
Peel the cucumber, thinly cut in half lengthways, scoop out and discard the seeds. Chop the flesh finely and place between several layers of kitchen towel. Press hard to remove as much moisture as possible. Transfer the squeezed cucumber to a bowl, add the remaining ingredients, and mix until well blended. Serve chilled with Greek bread or with souvlaki.

Theepless

Serves 4

Ingredients
4 tablespoons sugar
4 eggs
grated zest of 1 lemon
2 tablespoons vegetable oil
14 ounces self-raising flour
oil for deep frying

For the coating:
12 ounces honey
8 ounces sugar
cinnamon
coarsely chopped walnuts (optional)

Directions
In a mixing bowl, beat together the eggs, sugar, lemon zest, and oil. Place the flour in a large mixing bowl and make a well in the center. Pour the egg mixture in the well then, using your hands, gradually combine the mixture. Knead the dough until firm. Divide the dough into fourths.

On a lightly floured surface and using a floured rolling pin, roll out each portion into a paper-thin square. Cut the rolled out dough portions into 4 triangles.

Heat the oil to 350°F. Carefully place one triangle into the hot oil. As soon as it turns pale and bubbly, quickly remove from the oil and, using two large forks, roll into a cylindrical

shape. Set aside. Repeat with the remaining triangles.

When all of the triangles have been cooked,
return the oil to 350°F, and return the rolled up
triangles to the oil and cook until golden brown.
Remove from the oil and drain well on paper
towels. Let cool. Meanwhile, place the honey
and sugar in a saucepan and heat until boiling,
spooning off any froth that forms.

To serve, place the pastries on a serving
platter, drizzle the honey syrup over the top,
and sprinkle with the cinnamon and walnuts if
desired.

Baklava

Crushed nuts in a phyllo pastry topped with
syrup.

Ingredients
7/8 lb ground almonds or walnuts
1 cup butter
2 teaspoons cinnamon
1 pinch clove (to taste)
1 pound phyllo pastry dough
1 tablespoon lemon juice
2 cups sugar
1 cup honey
2 teaspoons vanilla
1 1/2 cups water

Directions
Mix the almonds, cinnamon, and cloves. Butter
a pan and place 4 buttered sheets of phyllo.
Spread a thin layer of the mix and then two
more sheets of phyllo. Repeat until you have 4
sheets left, which you use for the top layer. Cut
the baklava in squares, all the way to the bottom of the pan.

Top with the remaining butter and bake in
350°F oven for 45 minutes.

Mix the sugar, honey, vanilla, lemon juice
and 1 1/2 cups of water in a pot and boil for 5
minutes.

Remove any froth off the top and pour over
the baklava. Serve cold.

Salata Marouli (Romaine Lettuce Salad)

Serves 6

Ingredients
2–3 tablespoons fresh dill, chopped
1 head Romaine lettuce
pinch of salt
3–4 scallions, chopped
1/2 cup olive oil (more or less, depending on your own taste)
1/4 cup vinegar (more or less, depending on your own taste)

Directions
In a jar with a lid, combine the olive oil, vinegar, and salt. Put on lid and shake the jar well. Test for tartness (this dressing is usually more tart). Set aside.

Under cold, running water, wash the lettuce leaves and scallions well. Chop the lettuce finely and place in a large salad bowl. Add the scallions and the dill. When ready to serve, shake the salad dressing again, and pour on salad to taste.

NOTE: Add croutons and sliced hard-boiled eggs for variety.

Project and Report Ideas

Maps

- Make a map of the eurozone, and create a legend to indicate key manufacturing industries throughout the EU.
- Create an export map of Greece using a legend to represent all the major products exported by Greece. The map should clearly indicate all of Greece's industrial regions.

Reports

- Write a brief report on Greece's agriculture.
- Write a report on Greece's concerns within the EU.
- Write a brief report on any of the following historical events:
  the Greek Dark Ages
  the Turkish rule of Greece
  World War II
- Research and write a report on the history of the Olympic Games in Greece

Biographies
Write a one-page biography on one of the following:

- Homer
- Alexander the Great
- Sappho
- Nikos Kazantzakis

Journals

- Imagine you are a student in Greece who is finishing primary school. Write a journal debating whether to continue your education. You should include the decision you make and the reasons for that decision.
- Read more about the German occupation of Greece during World War II. Imagine you are a Jew living during that time. Write a journal describing what is happening and if you receive help from the Greek Orthodox Church.

Projects

- Learn the Greek expressions for simple words such as hello, good day, please, thank you. Try them on your friends.
- Make a calendar of your country's festivals and list the ones that are common or similar in Greece. Are they celebrated differently in Greece? If so, how?
- Go online or to the library and find images of the Parthenon or the Acropolis. Create a model of one of them.
- Make a list of all the places, seas, and islands that you have read about in this book and indicate them on a map of Greece.
- Find a Greek recipe other than the ones given in this book, and ask an adult to help you make it. Share it with members of your class.

Group Activities

- Debate: One side should take the role of Greece and the other Germany. Greece's position is that the EU should adopt an intergovernmental approach, while Germany will speak in favor of supra-nationalism.
- Act out a scene in Homer's *The Odyssey*.

CHRONOLOGY

3000 BCE	The Minoans arrive in Greece.
1600 BCE	Mycenaeans invade Greece; the Bronze Age begins.
1100 BCE	The Bronze Age ends.
1100–700 BCE	The Dark Ages envelop Greece.
776 BCE	The first Olympic Games are held.
497–479 BCE	The Persian Wars are fought.
461–445 BCE	The first Peloponnesian War occurs.
431–404 BCE	The second Peloponnesian War is fought.
323 BCE	Alexander the Great dies.
146 BCE	Greece is annexed into the Roman Empire.
395 CE	The Byzantine Empire is formed.
1453	The Byzantine Empire falls to the Ottomans.
1812	The Greeks begin to fight for independence.
1829	The Greeks win their independence from the Turks.
1940	Italy invades Greece.
1949	The Greek civil war is fought.
1967	The Regime of the Colonels begins.
1974	An election leads to the disbanding of the monarchy.
1975	A democratic constitution goes into effect.
1981	Greece joins the EU.
2001	Greece adopts the euro.

FURTHER READING/INTERNET RESOURCES

Greenblatt, Miriam. *Alexander the Great and Ancient Greece*. New York: Benchmark Books, 2000.
Heinrichs, Ann, and Amy J. Johnson. *Greece*. New York: Scholastic Library, 2001.
Nardo, Don. *Ancient Greece*. Farmington Hills, Mich.: Gale Group, 2000.
Nardo, Don. *Women of Ancient Greece*. San Diego, Calif.: Lucent.

Travel Information
www.greek-tourism.gr

History and Geography
www.ancientgreece.com
www.historyforkids.org

Culture and Festivals
www.lonelyplanet.com/destinations/europe/greece/culture.htm
www1.greece.gr/ABOUT_GREECE/CountryProfile/about_profile_Cultural_Life%20.htm

Economic and Political Information
earthtrends.wri.org/text/economics-business/country-profile-73.html
www.hri.org/cgi-bin/brief?/nodes/grpol.html

EU Information
europa.eu.int

FOR MORE INFORMATION

Consulate General of Greece
69 East 79th Street
New York, NY 10021
Tel.: 212-988-5500

Embassy of Greece
2221 Massachusetts Avenue NW
Washington, DC 20008
Tel.: 202-939-5800

Embassy of the United States
91 Vasilissis Sophias Avenue
Athens 10160 Greece
Tel.: 30-210-721-2951

U.S. Department of State
2201 C Street NW
Washington, DC 20520
Tel.: 202-642-4000

GLOSSARY

annexed: Took over territory and incorporated it into another political body.

archaeologists: Scientists who study ancient cultures through the examination of their material remains.

archipelagos: Groups of islands.

autonomous: Politically independent and self-governing.

biodiversity: The range of organisms present in a particular ecological community.

blocs: United groups of countries.

Bronze Age: A historical period between 3500 and 1500 BCE, characterized by the use of tools made of bronze.

capital: Wealth in the form of property or money.

city-states: Independent states consisting of a sovereign city and its surrounding territory.

communists: Supporters of the political and economic theory in which all property and wealth is owned by all the members of a community.

compulsory: Required.

coup: The sudden overthrow of a government and seizure of political power.

deforestation: The removal of trees from an area of land.

diversity: A variety of something.

domestic: Produced, distributed, sold, or occurring within a country.

entrepreneurial: Relating to the setting up and financing of a commercial enterprise.

epics: Lengthy narrative poems.

excise: Government-imposed tax on a domestic good.

exile: Forced to live in another country.

exploit: Use, take advantage of.

fault line: A feature of the Earth's surface, occurring where displaced rock layers have broken through the Earth's surface.

fauna: The animal life of a particular region.

gross domestic product (GDP): The total value of all goods and services produced within a country in a year, minus net income from investments in other countries.

homogeneous: Consisting of the same kind of elements.

intricacy: Complex, with many details.

liberalize: To make less strict.

moderates: Makes milder, without extremes.

ostracized: Shunned, cast out from contact with others.

Phoenicians: Members of an ancient people who occupied Phoenicia, in present-day Syria.

prehistoric: Relating to the period before history was first recorded in writing.

ratified: Officially approved.

solidarity: To stand together in unity.

stagnancy: A period of inactivity.

tariff: A government-imposed tax on imports.

Thebans: Those who lived in the ancient Greek city of Thebes, northwest of present-day Athens.

tribute: Payment made by one ruler or state to another as a sign of submission.

INDEX

PICTURE CREDITS

BIOGRAPHIES

AUTHOR

Kim Etingoff currently lives in Vestal, New York, where she has lived for most of her life. She contributes to a small local newspaper, where she holds the position of editor in chief. A recent trip to Europe helped to foster her interest in other countries, cultures, and peoples.

SERIES CONSULTANTS

Ambassador John Bruton served as Irish Prime Minister from 1994 until 1997. As prime minister, he helped turn Ireland's economy into one of the fastest-growing in the world. He was also involved in the Northern Ireland Peace Process, which led to the 1998 Good Friday Agreement. During his tenure as Ireland's prime minister, he also presided over the European Union presidency in 1996 and helped finalize the Stability and Growth Pact, which governs management of the euro. Before being named the European Commission Head of Delegation in the United States, he was a member of the convention that drafted the European Constitution, signed October 29, 2004.

The European Commission Delegation to the United States represents the interests of the European Union as a whole, much as ambassadors represent their countries' interests to the U.S. government. Matters coming under European Commission authority are negotiated between the commission and the U.S. administration.